Charles & Diana

A Royal Family Album

Charles & Diana

A Royal Family Album

Photographs by

TIM GRAHAM

SUMMIT BOOKS

New York London Toronto Sydney Tokyo Singapore

For Eileen, Lucy and Tom

———————

SUMMIT BOOKS
Simon & Schuster Building
Rockefeller Center
1230 Avenue of the Americas
New York, New York 10020

Photographs copyright © 1991 by Tim Graham

Originally published in Great Britain by
Michael O'Mara Books Ltd, London

Designed by Yvonne Dedman
Quality printing and binding by
Printer Industria Grafica SA, Barcelona, Spain

10 9 8 7 6 5 4 3 2 1

Library of Congress cataloguing and publication data
available upon request

ISBN 0-671-74397-X

———————

Frontispiece: A family group at Highgrove.
Title page: An afternoon at a polo match.

Contents

A Royal Romance

Above: The start of the honeymoon cruise in Gibraltar.
Opposite: Engagement day at Buckingham Palace.

*'I've met all Prince Charles' girlfriends,
and you're streets ahead of all of 'em. If he
doesn't marry you, he's out of his tiny mind.'*

ARTHUR EDWARDS
(*The Sun* photographer, speaking to Lady Diana on her doorstep)

'That enchanting
teenager with the
chubby cheeks and frilly,
flounced skirts . . .'

JUDY WADE (author and journalist)

At the Young England Kindergarten
in September 1980.

In Nepal, 1980.

At Balmoral, 1981.

'I am amazed that she's been brave enough to take me on.'

THE PRINCE OF WALES

'I am absolutely delighted, thrilled, blissfully happy. I never had any doubts.'

LADY DIANA SPENCER

With Harvey.

'*With Prince Charles beside me I cannot go wrong.*'

LADY DIANA SPENCER

Above: First visit to Tetbury, Highgrove's local town, as a royal fiancée.

'*When I'm nervous I tend to giggle.*'

THE PRINCESS OF WALES

Laughing at photographers in Hampshire, May 1981.

'In Diana's early months of public life the strain of her new-found position as the world's most famous woman told, and only by an enormous effort of will did she cope with the unbearable attention and lack of privacy.'

ALAN HAMILTON
(author and journalist)

Leaving a charity gala at Goldsmith's Hall, London after the first official appearance together.

A quiet moment during hectic Royal Ascot Week.

Leaving St Paul's Cathedral
after a wedding rehearsal, July 1981.

*'Our wedding was quite
extraordinary as far as
we were concerned. It
made us both extra-
ordinarily proud to be
British.'*

THE PRINCE OF WALES

'When you marry in my position, you're going to marry someone who, perhaps, is one day going to be Queen. You've got to choose somebody very carefully, I think, who could fulfil this particular role, and it has got to be somebody pretty unusual.'

THE PRINCE OF WALES

Above: After the marriage service.

Left: The first curtsey as a princess.

'You look wonderful.'

THE PRINCE OF WALES

'Wonderful for you.'

THE PRINCESS OF WALES

Above: The honeymoon in Gibraltar starts with a wave.

'I *can highly recommend it. It is a marvellous life.*'
THE PRINCESS OF WALES

Britannia reaches the Suez Canal.

The cruise ends at Hurghada in Egypt.

'We expected that, following the honeymoon, press attention would wane somewhat, but it has in no way abated.'

MICHAEL SHEA (the Queen's press secretary)

The honeymoon continues at Balmoral.

At the Grand National Meeting at Aintree near Liverpool in April 1982.

With friends at Aintree.

'Theirs is a partnership, and it works.'

SIR ALASTAIR BURNET (author and broadcaster)

Below: Shortly before Prince William's birth.

Presenting the first prize at a polo match in aid of Birthright in 1985.

*'I think she's a lovely
girl and we're all lucky
to have her.'*

EARL SPENCER (father of the
Princess of Wales)

Overleaf: An extra prize from the
prizewinner after a polo match in 1985.

The early days on tour, Cape Spear in Canada.

'*We both have the same sense of humour.*'

THE PRINCESS OF WALES

Below: An afternoon of polo.

'*Great fun and full of life.*'

THE PRINCE OF WALES (about his wife)

Opposite: Posing for photographers while skiing at Klosters in Switzerland in 1986.

Above: On tour in Melbourne, Australia.

'*She's a delightful girl. Charles could not find a more perfect partner.*'

THE QUEEN

'*Attractive, wholesome, agreeably shy without being silly, she is every mother's idea of the sort of girl they would like their sons to marry.*'

ROBERT LACEY (author)

Just before Prince Harry's birth in 1984.

Watching a dancing display
during the tour of Australia in 1983.

*'The chubby-cheeked
blonde with the chunky
hairdo vanished . . . a
more stylish, more
confident woman stands
by the side of Prince
Charles today. It says a
lot for her steely
determination that she
has come through a
period of awesome
adjustment and
emerged more dazzling
than ever.'*

JUDY WADE (author and journalist)

A nautical look for a visit to the Italian navy
at La Spezia, in 1985.

A Family

Above: A helping hand from his brother for Prince Harry's first steps.
Opposite: A family group among the wildflowers at Highgrove.

'It's an affectionate family
under perpetual public scrutiny.'

SIR ALASTAIR BURNET (author and broadcaster)

'I always feel he will be all right because he has been born to his royal role. He will get accustomed to it gradually.'

THE PRINCESS OF WALES
(on Prince William)

'The birth of our son has given us both more pleasure than you can imagine. It has made me incredibly proud and somewhat amazed.'

THE PRINCE OF WALES

Opposite: With the young Prince William.

Prince William at the photocall in Auckland, New Zealand in 1983.

Above: A piano duet at Kensington Palace.

Helping Prince William with his jigsaws in the day room at Kensington Palace.

'He's not at all shy but very polite ...'

THE PRINCESS OF WALES
(on Prince William)

'... Harry is quieter ... he's certainly a different character altogether.'

THE PRINCESS OF WALES

Opposite: With Prince Harry in Majorca.

With one-year-old Prince Harry in the drawing-room at Kensington Palace.

'He is a doting daddy and does everything perfectly.'

THE PRINCESS OF WALES (on Prince Charles as a father)

Early start for a public role.

Enjoying family life at Kensington Palace, 1985.

Prince William joins his father at the Guards Polo Club, Windsor.

A reassuring hand from father for Prince Harry.

Arriving at Aberdeen airport.

A goodbye kiss at polo.

'My husband knows so much about rearing children that I've suggested he has the next one and I'll sit back and give advice.'

THE PRINCESS OF WALES

'Paratroopers' at Highgrove.

Above: Prince Harry's first day at Wetherby.
Below: On board *Britannia* in Venice, 1985.

Left: The family at Highgrove
and *(inset)* Prince William with Smokey.

In the grounds of Highgrove.

'*They are normal little boys, who are unlucky enough to create an abnormal amount of attention.*'

THE PRINCE OF WALES

Right: On the terrace at Highgrove.

Prince William taking part in his first carriage procession at Trooping the Colour.

Taking Prince William to school.

'*William is a splendid little character, and very good-natured. He seems to have quite a good sense of humour. And he is very outgoing.*'

THE PRINCE OF WALES

Having left Prince Harry at school.

An informal salute at Highgrove.

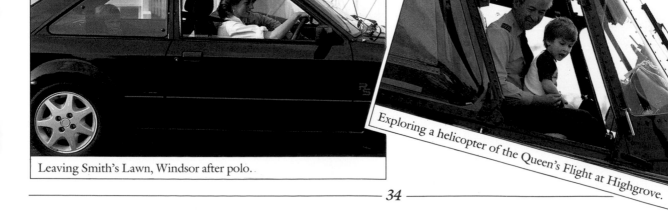

Leaving Smith's Lawn, Windsor after polo.

Exploring a helicopter of the Queen's Flight at Highgrove.

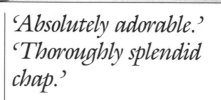

'Absolutely adorable.'
'Thoroughly splendid chap.'

THE PRINCE OF WALES
(on Prince Harry)

In high spirits on the balcony of Buckingham Palace.

Holding the new pet rabbit, watched by his parents.

'Harry is the mischievous one.'

THE PRINCESS OF WALES

Opposite: At Highgrove.

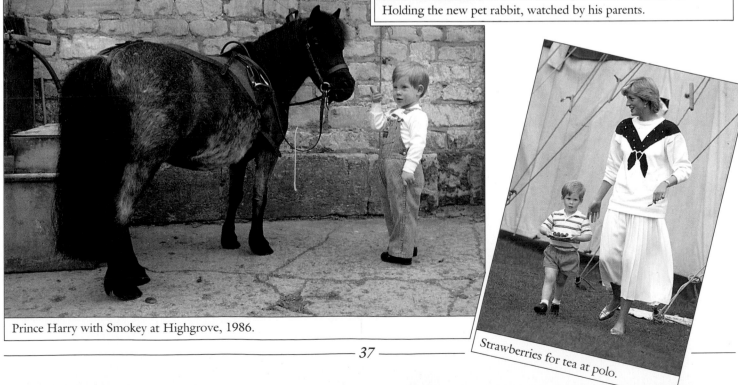

Prince Harry with Smokey at Highgrove, 1986.

Strawberries for tea at polo.

Roving Ambassadors

Above: Passports.
Opposite: The first royal tour for a new princess.

'*Charles and Diana are mirrors and exemplars of stalwart British qualities: civility, courtesy and coziness, with a dash of style and a bit of fun.*'

TIME (magazine, USA)

A gallant gesture in Melbourne, Australia.

Left: A rainy welcome in Wales for its new princess.

Enjoying a laugh with the locals in Loughborough, Leicestershire in April 1990.

'It would have been far easier to have had two wives to have covered both sides of the street. And I could have walked down the middle directing the operation.'

THE PRINCE OF WALES

Enthusiastic crowds on a walkabout in Milan in 1985.

In Berlin as Colonel-in-Chief of the Royal Hampshire Regiment.

Opposite: In a borrowed naval cap during a visit to a nuclear submarine.

Waiting to greet King Fahd of Saudi Arabia.

'One of the more glamorous Colonels-in-Chief of the British Army.'

THE PRINCE OF WALES (about his wife)

Ready for a driving lesson in a 15-ton armoured personnel carrier with the Hampshires in Berlin.

At Trooping the Colour
as Colonel of the Welsh Guards.

'I would change-nothing.
Besides ceremony being
a major and important
aspect of monarchy,
something that has
grown and developed
over a thousand years in
Britain, I happen to
enjoy it enormously.'

THE PRINCE OF WALES (on
ceremonial duties)

The Great Master of the Order of the Bath.

Above: Returning to Windsor Castle
by carriage after the Garter Day Service.

'There is no more fitting
preparation for a king
than to have been
trained in the navy.'

PRINCE LOUIS OF BATTENBERG

Left: Naval uniform on Veterans' Day at
the Arlington National Cemetery, Virginia.
Right: Investiture at Buckingham Palace.
Overleaf: Visiting Cameroon in West Africa.

'To be modern, yet keep the mystique — that is the trick. It is a trick that Charles and Diana have gracefully mastered.'

TIME magazine, USA

A traditional Maori greeting in New Zealand in 1983.

Being installed as an island chief in Papua New Guinea.

'*People expect a great deal of us . . .*'

THE PRINCE OF WALES

Safety hats raise a giggle in Australia.

Klondike fancy dress in Canada.

In a Maori war canoe on an official tour of New Zealand in 1983.

Visiting a temple in India.

'. . . *a sense of humour is what keeps me sane and I would probably have been committed to an institution long ago were it not for the ability to see the funny side of life.*'

THE PRINCE OF WALES

A visit to Hong Kong in 1989.

Drinking from a coconut while on tour in India.

Opposite: Dinner at the British Embassy in Washington in 1985 and *(inset)* with the Vice-President and Mrs Bush.

'I assure you it makes the heart sink to have to make an awful exhibition of ourselves.'

PRINCE OF WALES (on dancing)

Left: Dancing in Melbourne, Australia during bicentennial celebrations.

'Imagine having to go to a wedding every day of your life — as the bride. Well, that's a bit what it's like.'

THE PRINCESS OF WALES (on official engagements)

Tiara check during a banquet in New Zealand, 1983.

'If you haven't got an invite, the best idea is to leave town and pretend your mother is ill.'

AN AMERICAN SOCIALITE (on parties for the Prince and Princess of Wales in Washington, 1985)

Visiting the Peto Institute, Budapest.

'I think she likes children because she is always bending down to talk and whisper secrets.'

SIMON LIU (aged 6, writing to *Majesty* magazine)

Talking to a physically handicapped child during a visit to the Markfield Project in London, 1986.

At a British Deaf Association conference.

A leprosy hospital, Indonesia.

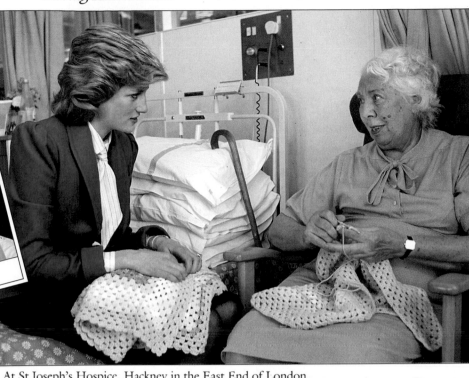

At St Joseph's Hospice, Hackney in the East End of London.

Greeting an old lady in London.

'She's wonderful with people, especially the elderly and the young. She knows, instinctively, how to put them at their ease. And she has compassion — she's not afraid to shake hands with either an AIDS patient or a leper.'

PHILIPPA KENNEDY (journalist)

With an HIV positive child.

Proficient in sign language.

Blowing out the candles at Barnardo's.

Making a speech in the Shetland Isles in 1986.

'His ideas are sound, his heart is in the right place and he has a remarkable gift for communicating with the man in the street and understanding his needs. Furthermore, he cares about those needs, and has the clout among businessmen and politicians to make mountains move.'

PENNY JUNOR (author)

Visiting a Prince's Trust project in Manchester.

Making a visit to the ultra-modern and controversial Pyramide du Louvre in Paris, 1988.

'The first function of any monarchy is the human concern for people . . .'

THE PRINCE OF WALES

A spontaneous welcome in Liverpool.

An animated conversation with nurses at a hospital in Liverpool.

Right: A desert picnic at an oasis in Abu Dhabi in 1989.

'*I'm just a roving ambassador for Britain.*'

THE PRINCE OF WALES

Above: Seeing traditional life during a visit to Indonesia in 1989.

'*The Princess of Wales has done more to popularise the concept of monarchy throughout the world than any other member of the Royal Family in the last ten years.*'

DOUGLAS KEAY (author and journalist)

Returning from a drive through the Hungarian countryside in a horse-drawn carriage in 1990.

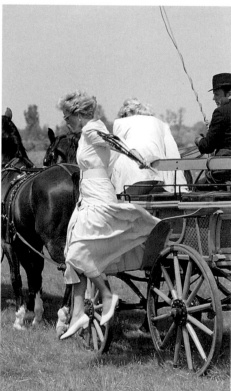

Meeting Nigerian women in local costume during an official visit in 1990.

Playing bowls in Indonesia, 1989.

Arriving in Melbourne for an official visit.

Private Lives

Above: Joking with the crowd at polo.
Opposite: At polo with Prince William in 1988.

'The fascination of a constitutional monarchy
to its people will always be less to do with
a Prince's role than what, if anything,
he wears in bed.'

ANTHONY HOLDEN (author)

'Very therapeutic, weeding, and it's marvellous if you can do it enough to see the effect.'

THE PRINCE OF WALES

Right: A quiet moment in the grounds of Highgrove.

Weeding in the gardens at Highgrove.

In the gardens at Highgrove where the family relaxes at weekends.

Negotiating a steep run at Klosters.

Preparing for action.

> '*I believe very strongly that moral courage can come from an experience of physical danger.*'
>
> THE PRINCE OF WALES

Presenting a new face at Klosters.

Clowning on the slopes with the Duchess of York.

Togetherness on the ski lift.

A stylish descent.

Polo has always been a favourite recreation and the family are keen supporters.

'*I love the game. I love the ponies. I love the exercise.*'

THE PRINCE OF WALES (on polo)

On holiday with the Spanish and Greek royal families.

'*These days it is a classier version of the traditional bucket-and-spade holiday which attracts the Princess.*'

ANDREW MORTON (author and journalist)

Opposite: An idyllic holiday on Necker in the Caribbean.

A weekend in Spain.

With Queen Sophia's puppy.

The King of Spain and Prince William.

A cuddle for Prince Harry at the photocall in Majorca.

'I am not exhibiting my sketches because I am under the delusion that they represent great art or burgeoning talent. They represent my particular form of photographic album, and as such mean a great deal to me.'

THE PRINCE OF WALES

Sketching in the gardens of
the Imperial Palace, Kyoto during
an official tour of Japan.

'*It has come as a
pleasant surprise to find
that at least one son has
a real talent for water-
colour.*'

THE DUKE OF EDINBURGH

Opposite: In the drawing-room at Kensington Palace, 1985.

Above: In the sitting-room at Kensington Palace.

'*Charles and Diana are arguably the most famous, the most glamorous couple in the world.*

TIME magazine, USA

'*She has saved the tradition of dressing up.*'

DAVID EMANUEL (designer)

Discussions with dress designer David Emanuel in preparation for an overseas tour.

Left: Riding at Badminton and *(inset)* swimming at Bondi Beach, Australia.

> '*If there was anything left to discover in the world, Charles would have been an explorer.*'

THE QUEEN MOTHER

Right: Trekking in the Himalayan foothills.

Visiting the Korup in Cameroon in 1990, one of the largest protected areas of natural rainforest in the world.

A Sense of Style

Above: An official photograph at Kensington Palace in 1983.
Opposite: Paying a compliment to Japan in 1986.

'In the nicest possible way
she is well aware that she is a dish.'

CLIVE JAMES (author and broadcaster)

'She would even look
good in a sack.'
PRINCESS MICHAEL OF KENT

'*She is genuinely
beautiful. I don't know
why she needs me really.*'

BARBARA DALY (make-up artist)

Right: On the front steps of Highgrove.

At Clarence House for the Queen Mother's 90th birthday.

In the cockpit before a helicopter trip around Highgrove.

In Westminster.

The school run.

With Viscount Linley at Royal Ascot in 1990.

At the Derby in 1987 with the Duchess of York.

Off-duty in London.

Taking Prince William to school.

'It could be something as simple as the way she belts an outfit or the way she wears a scarf, but whatever it is, it always looks elegantly different on Diana — somehow more distinctive and stylish.'

INGRID SEWARD (editor, *Majesty*)

Matching red accessories for an afternoon of polo at Cirencester.

Above: An embroidered look with pearls.

Diamonds with velvet
for the banquet in Bonn
in 1987.

Above: Satin and lace for a gala at Sadler's Wells.
Opposite: A bold design for this evening dress.

'*The Princess is quite thrifty
with clothes. They often come back
and we remodel them, shorten
them or restyle them. But if we
cut them in shreds they would
still look spectacular on her.*'

VICTOR EDELSTEIN (dress designer)

'. . . you can't have anything too revealing. And you can't have hems too short because when you bend over there are six children looking up your skirt! Clothes are for the job. They've got to be practical.'

THE PRINCESS OF WALES

Cameras at the ready to record each arrival, the choice of outfit always attracts comment.

Garlanded with flowers in Papua New Guinea.

'I do so like men in uniform.'

THE PRINCESS OF WALES

Visiting the Indian Parachute Regiment Brigade Headquarters.

As Colonel of the Welsh Guards on St David's Day in Surrey.

Colonel-in-Chief of the 2nd King Edward VII Own Goorkhas.

Naval uniform for the Remembrance Day Service at the Cenotaph in London.

'*We're very lucky as she has a terrific face for hats. There are so many large-brimmed shapes which she looks tremendous in . . .*'

PHILIP SOMERVILLE (milliner)

'*Hats give me confidence.*'

THE PRINCESS OF WALES

Lilac silk for the ballet in Auckland, New Zealand on the first official tour.

Mauve crushed velvet for a Barnardo's gala.

'It was one of the things I always noticed about her before we got married. She had, I thought, a very good sense of style and design.'

THE PRINCE OF WALES

Red and gold for a film première.

Silk and pearls at the Victoria and Albert Museum in 1981.

In Washington, 1985.

In Washington, 1990.

Taffeta and velvet for the opera in Munich.

Arriving for a banquet at the British Embassy in Paris, 1988.

Entering the Hungarian Parliament in Budapest for a Presidential banquet, 1990.

'Her faithful patronage has almost single-handedly revived the flagging British high-fashion industry.'

NEWSWEEK magazine, USA

Attending a performance of *Swan Lake* in London, 1988.

'The Princess of Wales knows that if clothes are going to talk, less says more.'

LOUETTE HARDING
(*Sunday Express* magazine)

Opposite: At the première of *Dangerous Liaisons* and *(inset)* in Hong Kong.
Overleaf: At the Cannes Film Festival, 1987.

'*She has not only become perhaps the most famous and most frequently photographed woman in the world, but she has helped to bring the institution of monarchy to a new peak of popularity and boosted the image of Britain worldwide.*'

PENNY JUNOR (author)

Walking through the streets of Budapest during the tour of Hungary in 1990.